Montréal Undecided

Montréal Undecided
by Lis McLoughlin

ISBN: 978-1-960293-22-0
First Edition

Montréal Undecided

by
Lis McLoughlin

Published by
NatureCulture
Northfield, MA
and
Montréal, QC

Montréal Undecided
Table of Contents

Preface

Intentions

Transactions

Arrival

Observations: Deux Villes

Montréal Eats

Scruffy in a Chic City

A Year later

Dreams/Rêves

Epilogue

Poetry comes down to:
Life is not what I thought it could be
or
It is so much more.

PREFACE

The geometric version of nature that urban dwellers prefer

Montréal is a hard city—stone, metal, pavement. Green spaces, yes, but contained, starved for water, scented with urine, littered with unwanteds. Every morning, and throughout the day, teams of people put together the city; and every day and throughout the night, teams dismantle it. Flower boxes with outrageous displays of riotous color flora are planted and watered, and then ripped up along the edges, to be swept up and rearranged slightly to disguise the holes. In winter these boxes hold artfully arranged birch logs, evergreen boughs, and fairy lights, and sometimes styled bushes—plain white cones lit from inside. People seem to like these cousins of the orange cones that attempt to keep us out of potholes and other dangers.

Sticks-in-pots is a major Montréal theme. Corners of condos, restaurants, and storefronts are marked with potted sticks, and in bathrooms their miniature versions disperse essential oils to combat negative scents. Some restaurants extend their flora around the doorway itself, making the entrance feel like a secret garden gate, with vines clutching at capes and hair, and promising fresh produce inside, artfully prepared—which there usually is. How they receive fresher greens than I can get living next to the farm itself I don't know, but somebody must know somebody else, or else, urban gardening really is a thing. There are 45,000 independent farmers in Quebec, and 5 in Northfield where I live the rest of the year. When I go back I will see real trees, messy unlit bushes, and sticks without pots; but I will miss eating the artfully arranged fresh lettuce.

INTENTIONS

I imagine a home
where I can be myself
And I am defeated
because either I have never known myself
or I have never known that home

Our mistakes are not going to follow us to Montréal. The towels we almost liked and were on sale, the boots that turned out not to be quite waterproof, the keyboard that doesn't save your wrists from aching but does look funny and take up a lot of room on your desk.

No socks with holes.
No dishes with fussy cleaning requirements.
No fitted sheets that don't stay firmly attached at the corners.
We are not bringing our old, tired, weary, or odd-shaped.

Laminate, knobbly, read once and didn't like much, or uncomfortable to write with.
Half dead plants, half burned tunnelled candles, and art that makes no emotional impression upon me any more all stay here.

Books I haven't read yet or written, and the coloured pens to write them with, the pottery mugs to hold rich coffee, the wool throw I snuggle under each day, and slippers. And good walking boots, and a warm hat.

New candles. New lights. New art and pans and plates.

My good cherry desk I never put in the attic nook. My thin irascible cat whose unpredictable purrs make my day.

TRANSACTIONS

US exchange rate for $24,000:
Universal 1.3210
Globex 1.3135
Scotiabank: 1.22879

I am giving directions to my realtor. "There is construction, but you can get through that street anyway."

"If there wasn't construction, it wouldn't be Montréal." he replies.

He didn't last the length of our first meeting as my realtor—honestly, what good realter needs directions in his own territory?

~

"I saw a huge fish jump up in the canal this morning" I said to my new realtor.

"I didn't know anything lived there" she replied.

ARRIVAL

The phrase from Duolingo which I can't get correct is: "J'ai eu beaucoup de difficultes a me faire comprendre."

Clearly the apartment had been staged
the young woman who sold it to us
(she was young, her mother was the realtor)
had as one of her few books
The subtle art of not giving a f*ck

What I can't do without land

- compost
- let homeless sleep there
- graze sheep
- put up a fence to keep people and noises and cars farther away from me
- ride my atv
- see the sunrise/set
- grow food
- collect defunct vehicles
- build large sculptures
- grow a tree

25 May 2021

Dear co-owner,

With the arrival of nice weather the terrace is now officially open. In order for ALL residents to enjoy the terrace please take a moment to read the following excerpts of the syndicate bylaw.

The terrace is open and accessible from 21:30 to 23:00. *It is forbidden for any person to be present on the terrace outside these hours. Including you. We are not falling for that "need access to dark skies to practice my reũgion" shit. This is Ville-Marie, not Ville-Sasquatch.*

Access to and use of the terrace might be controlled by security cameras, occasionally by an officer of a surveillance company, and those robot things they have at Walmart.

All costs incurred (manager intervention and increased bar tab to calm ensuing headache, concierge and associated cleaning supplies including vomit surcharge) will be charged to the co-owner of the residential unit whose residents and/or guests (including teenagers, toddlers, and hockey fans) have caused damage.

Pets are strictly prohibited on the terrace.
It is forbidden to listen to music without headphones.
It is forbidden to listen to the CBC even with headphones.
It is forbidden to set foot and / or walk, wade, aquacise, or immerse any part of your body, sun-baked or otherwise, in the water basin. Also, do not deposit your aquatic or other pets into the water basin.
It is forbidden to circulate on any section of the roof outside the area bounded by the tile floor and the metal rail guards where the dragon lives.
It is mandatory to clean grills and close the gas supply located on the wall after use. If you're cooking steak, bring enough for everybody.
It is mandatory to clean and replace the tables, chairs, and pigeons at the locations indicated on the plan after use.

An additional fee of TWO HUNDRED FIFTY DOLLARS ($ 250) per event date will be charged the co-owner of the offending unit.

We also ask you to be discreet in hallways and stairs when you access the terrace. Don't let your significant other see you sneaking up there with someone else. **If applicable please advise your tenants.**

Thank you for your cooperation,

~

Last night the upstairs neighbours seem to have adopted an elephant, a
toddler, and a cat.

~

Is the condo manager my husband now? Can I complain to M. Marois
about a cricket? It's a noise, but it's not mechanical. Are crickets
natural in the city? Are they to be expected? If yes, then what about
silverfish? Rats? The raccoon I saw once crossing the road? The gull
that cruises these canyons of streets seasonally? My cat trapped indoors
behind glass? The dogs in the street whose poop is collected by their
owners and who mostly stay on leashes?

More horses walk by the condo window than our home in the country.
They pull carriages full of tourists. They have jobs just like everyone
else in the city.

~

Idea: put up a sign in the window: "Please smoke here under my window
so I can tell you about my grandchildren"

The square of sky is the palest blue

as if the sun bleached the tint
jealously
the white sunlight burns all before it
      harbinger of destruction
      harbinger of heat
      clarity of relentless oblivion

the sky is white today
and could I write upon it
like a page
with blue ink I would fill it end to end
and let its color
speak its life for itself.

OBSERVATIONS:
DEUX VILLES

I see a light reflected in an upper window
It could be the moon
or another window
with a light on in it.

This morning the Navy and Coast Guard are recruiting at the Old Port. From a bus.

Improved by Poetry

The thing is
that the space where you go to write poems
is invisible from the outside

People who live their lives in motion
with other people and money or love and jogging—
fashion
art
traffic
the state of the sidewalks
constantly in their minds

walk by these spaces
as blithely as they walk
by the homeless on the edges
of their own lives

While I walk doing errands
sometimes the place where I write poetry
will surprise me by opening
a boarded up door
and letting out the dust of sheetrock
or a stray cat
or music from another culture
or the odor of fried food I can't make at home
and I strain to capture it
before it drifts to imperceptibility
against the grey busy background
of accomplishing goals.
Or I let it pass by me
with a faint new smile
my day improved by a poetry

The Haze of Night

I am an expert at staying still
and hiding while the world goes by
prey praying my own secret thoughts
while they express every one of theirs
loudly, drunkenly into the dark.

The wee hours are mine
the witching hours
While they turn, turn, slowly
around the block in their midnight
black and luminous lunar white
vehicles not yet crashed by
drunken girlfriends into posts.

How do they survive
Night after night
walking on heels too small to
support the weight of their beauty
the light of intellect which
they hide by baring flesh and
stripping down to shiny bits of nothing
artfully arranged
conveniently easy to take off
if loyalty is questioned.

If loyalty is questioned it is out
loud, like all that happens here—
peeing, loving, stealing, smashing
glass—all laid bare
except those thoughts
buried under the noise and fog of drink
what are you thinking?

Monday Morning Montréal

The city unfolds glowing every night, then brings in her wings a sleepy bat, to expand again late morning to coffee and sun. I watch the furled sleep. Restless, exhausted, the human mites—the homeless run over the surface, crawl in and out of the creases picking up cigarette butts, dropping detritus.

Someone wants the bottles, rattling in the dead of night, death knells of parties, buoys marking channels of forgetting.

Someone else wants the metal, twisted among the cardboard, unfashionable chairs with one wheel missing, the alley an unmarked historic site where ephemera is created every day by worker bees in carrels, with ever decreasing attention spans, they dream up products with shorter and shorter lives.

Dogs pee on everything. Cars park on everything. Artificial light shines down benevolently and equally on it all.

When the clubs let out the beautiful losers spill into the streets in pairs in small groups, loud and full of piss they leave between cars and in doorways. On high heels, under sullen hoods they transit to vehicles they shouldn't drive, to apartments they shouldn't visit with people they shouldn't fuck.

In the stirrings of dawn, when a breeze ripples the hairs on the enfolded wings, they sleep an oblivion of relief. They will awaken dehydrated in the wrong clothes across town and arrange their faces into haughty francophone smirks—c'est normale. Home and late to work like everyone else, coffee in hand, footsteps on the trottoir barré keeping the Montréal bat flying white nosed into the future.

~

The mobile 'No Parking' signs are standing next to each other, a couple, facing out, which all Montréalers know means they aren't working and are doing the NoParking sign equivalent of smoking a fag.

~

The cars that go
the wrong way down my street
too fast (as if that makes it better)
never find parking anyway.

It's one of those pointless city games
the traffic plays with itself
until it snarls
or is straightened out by cones and men yelling
patrolling empty streets
gutters full of cars

~

Cab drivers are the sharks of the old port
seeking out the injured and forgotten
sweeping them off to the side.

Businessmanstone

A bald man
with a suit the color of stone
walks camouflaged before the building façades
in Rue Ste. Hélène
a gargoyle with a briefcase
jumped out of geological time in the morning light

Moving to a taller building on McGill
there to direct
less tangible—more potent—torrents' flow

Love leads us

Dust-coated the cars
as if they were in a time warp
as if 100 years had passed
out in the street
while we slept in air-conditioned
luxurious boxes.

The cars were still as alive as ever
their blue or red alarm-system
activation lights blinking
in sync with some electronic heartbeat
of their own
out of sync with one another
so that the night was full of blue
and red eyes hiding in the interiors of
metal burrows
eating the wires.

The dog walkers pass as if nothing
has changed
their little charges foraging
ahead into corners
alongside posts

while they text another human
and continue to ignore the canine
companion who only wants to
smell them and keep them safe
is ignorant of any other reality
besides this one
who has no choice but to live
in the moment
with or without you.

In the sunlight the gas lanterns
fade to superfluous but

no one turns them off—the
technology to do that has been lost
along with all the other skilled labor
that depended upon apprenticeship
—person teaching person—
hands passing knowledge to the next pair of hands
Over and over.
Too much was lost.

We thought machines could replace
the other humans' company
                        their expertise

yet the dogs, the dogs we don't think
can be replaced
so much simpler than a human
yet
love
love is the bond to a dog
                        to a family trade
                        to a tradition

Somewhere in the backs of our collective minds
we know love cannot be
replaced
even if we've forgotten how
to actually receive it.

Intermittently

People punctuate the space of the street
One moment crumpled posh
finding safe cars
to drive them home to safe condos
overlooking the city

Next moment
abject poverty
dirt, hair, stench

One moment the street is decorated with energy and hope
The next dragged down to its basest self

Both are true

They take turns creating realities
The outside observer changes
with the observing
Yet their trajectories never meet
separate slots for right and left handed destinies
one picking up the cigarette butts of the other
Like sharks the shiny ones don't mind remoras
Every psycho needs a sycophant

How much space can you afford

1 car's worth is $20 a day
1 room's worth is $1200 a month
1 human's worth depends where they are sitting
on the edge of the canal at a table $50/hour to eat
on the edge of the canal on the ground free and no food served

you can exist in space for only so long without food
It seems unfair to need to pay for both

Bonjour. Nod. Walk.

The beggars on Rue Ste Catherine
(patron saint of Not Them)
are so numerous they develop acts to grab your attention
One has a Maine coon cat and will show you his witch tattoo.
Another, a dog.
Another pretends to be retarded
"support the handicapped" he shakes his can in your face.

Any may be dismissed with a bonjour, a nod, a fast paced walk.
The hardest to shake greet you then say
Do you speak English? How are you?
Bonjour. Nod. Walk.

And I go home to my expensive box.
Outside my window an unhoused man stumbles drunkenly.
Inside, like a window display of things you don't want to buy/be
I am drunk on the couch.
There is only a pane of glass between us.
Bonjour.

Cycling

Before dawn
the homeless ride their bikes on the sidewalk
and pick up their cardboard mats from doorways.

Under the bridge they've tipped the
temporary construction fence so its banner creates a shelter
from the rain.
Under the chain link and poly
they sleep in puddles
until it's time to rise and walk
and ride
with the sun across the city
so rich with silver
the very least dribble of which sustains them all

Across from the bridge
The rain waters the garden plot
of the homeless Asian man
on the embankment
and reaches too
his sleeping friends

Even the rain barters here in the financial district
giving food
taking rest.

MONTRÉAL EATS

Bon appétit.

Brunch at Holder

is a CEO on family weekend vacation. Unbuttoned.

Wood walls, rare veal, whimsical art, fireplaces
Local drinks—anemic wine, robust waters—
Folded napkins, salad forks, a peppermill that never materializes—

women in black—
guarding goslings cappuccino mug in hand,
or else, like me, egrets perched alone on precariously tippy tall stools
at reassuringly elegant bar tables
dipping bills into mimosas good to the last drop

pulsing music of vibrant, edgy lives well-lived
full, in a late-rising town

Le Cartet

is queen of hearts
and the gallant gallic waiter, the king

'Your French is good'
makes me blush like a girl
and tip like an American—

   I know how to pay a compliment.

Da Emma: In praise of Stone working

As if composing the world isn't enough
it now holds in our immeubles
knickknacks
and fashionable ideas

Enhancing bonheur at lunch
with broken surfaces
that used to keep in, coldly, the bad women
and now form a backdrop for the lucky ones at their most lively

Who says Stone can't be kind

Perhaps it always did this
Perhaps the bad women felt lucky to have the lovely grey background
if nothing else

Parliament

Friendly
strange
someone mansplaining

Someone's version of what a pub is supposed to be

The Fatheaded Man

The fatheaded man
expands in space
knees wide on the couch
offering his crotch to the room

He refuses hearing aids
forced to come to him
our voices expanding around his
fragile ego like bubble wrap
like an extension of himself
his "answers" blasting back like carpet bombs
flattening our affects
our ideas
our individual identities
female fertile fields around
the stony mountain man cave.

In the cafe corner—the middle corner—
the room turns toxic—
too loud
too gauche
for this francophone nation
where the children gurgle and chirp
more quietly than
one American burp or fart

cups set down pointedly
in a porcelain
condemnation.

At Maggie Oakes

The espresso maker exhales
like a young woman
breathing desire
into his ear

And either sex
or java will ensue
and both are hot
and end bitter
satisfying on the tongue

Business Conviviale à Balsam Inn Table d'Hôte

in the heart of the city
sharp suits and sheaths
smiling "Salut toi!"
imbibe the countryside
So later, finding thyme in their teeth,
they remember there is love and wine
some reason to get on the treadmill
some contentment
because if these BMW people
whose lives are driven so fast, so hard
can't stop and become
anchored
by comfort food
turned haute cuisine
they would fly away
pulling the city behind them
careening into the global economy
without a trace of the past
and without a hope
for the distinctive creative future they promise.

Chez Delmo III: The Woman with the Rasp

She travels with an entourage
who suggest she sounds like a movie star

With any luck
the woman you want to be
is in a dress on a hanger
in the window of that store across the street

or she is
in a dress eating lunch
in the window of Chez Delmo

the woman with the man in the city suit
in your city dress

His is made for him
yours is made for him too—your
back, waist, thighs
—best parts—
on display
modesty in the rear view mirror of your
careening career trajectory

Now you smell expensive
in your hair, luxurious product
your body the sexiest suit you will ever own
as essential as high leather boots to click across marble floor
straight white teeth to smile at the world
the lace of your superfluous a-cups a welcome guest at the table

The man behind the bar and I
we both query desires

Aren't you going back to work this afternoon?

I am at work,
the poet
robed in words.

Men who want to talk to Me on the phone

Men who want to talk to Me on the phone,
can kiss my ass.

They suffer from being lumped in with all the men I've ever wanted to
talk to
who never called back

Men who want to talk to me on the phone
Are afflicted likewise with the legacy of all men who had rescue calls

Men who poked their head into restaurant
glanced at the blind date in her closet-crushed best
and ducked back out to disappear into the white noise of the rain

Through the rising, buzzing dial tone of anger
I become the woman at the bar who
caught his culpable reflection in the glass
and realized she was relieved

Untethered for the weekend
fired by good food,
excellent wine
attended by hot men in black
who are solicitous about my wellbeing—in the flesh.

Ignore the annoying ring tones
the connection problems
and the inconsistent.....service—

My phone is permanently off the hook.

Sitting Unserved at the bar in Montréal

I am afraid if I leave
I will leave my poetry here
and bereft without it
I will not really be living
while the music of the city
goes on without me having incorporated my essence

and when I return
I'll be too dissolute to find
or would have wandered elsewhere
to Mile Ex perhaps
or the gay village—to dance—
and won't be called home
to inhabit whatever shell is left

SCRUFFY
IN A
CHIC CITY

Yoga Intention:
I want to be happy being/doing me.

The calendar at the Luna Yoga studio says
"Karma Made Me Do It"

Observation:
There are trucks growling Ohm in the street

Fortune Smiles

Beauty is admired
in the moment
not only for its present presence
but also
for what it says
about how that woman lives her life.

Beauty is earned
as a body's moment passes
through every step on the treadmill
through brushing, flossing, straightening, whitening
through various Treatments
with various Products
through a cultivated habit of smiling
complacently
or complicitly
as the moment demands
year in year out.

But beauty is wild
built of tamed and disciplined moments
it shines out to all
a treacherous beacon
marking the owner for great sorrow
or success
depending upon her fortune

Justice is blind
Fortune is not

Yoga-ing While Fat

The young bodies flow
Standing
bent
standing
bent wider
standing wider
flat and hovering

I drag myself across my mat
like some swamp thing
twisted
forearms digging in

I raise my legs to the wall and rest
I breathe and try to convince myself this breath
is doing yoga
just
like
them.

~

The instructor suggests I take 2 spaces to have more room! Yay!

Insight: My body wants to be a full fat snake for her transition.
Intention: get unstuck
Intention: be kind to the woman I am
Instructor's t-shirt says "Pizza is my spirit animal" I can't get away.

If I can't replace my longing for food
with a longing for something else
I will die.

~

In Yoga, In Imagination: I have managed to call a flock of barred owls to me and they are helping by eating my imaginary food. I think they will enjoy yoga. They are perched in imaginary branches they manifested along the top edges of the walls. A few are on the ceiling fans trying to get them to work. Owls really love twists!

~

The calendar at yoga says "Let that shit go"

One Breath

One breath
is a full tide.
In
and Out.

How many years
is a full tide of life
blood, no blood, blood, no blood———

You can see where the idea of a return came from
          Next time I'll_____

I don't count on next time

There is no delayed gratification
there is only the pounding on the shore of
          NOW
          Now
          now......

A YEAR LATER

Conversational French class:
Aller faire—going to do

Guest towels are not far off

Over time, the house fills
not according to plan
with collections of little things
people give you because you like X
And jaunty little animal shapes
to relieve the tasteful black and white and wood

Would you give up the dream of who you thought you'd be
For a little happiness in the kitchen

List of things to buy (not crossed out):
-apron hook 3/4" width
-umbrella holder
-conditioner
-entry hall mirror/hook/wall thing
-bedside tables or cubes
-deskside file cabinet/end table
-knife sharpener
-laundry bags
-(maybe) jewellery box
-hair dryer
-rolly shopping cart

List of things to buy (crossed out):
-mittens
-jalapeno popcorn
-toner
-stamps to the US
-soft scrub
-note cards
-sharpie markers
-pencil cup
-Marimekko pot holders
-EQ3 table?
-ceiling fan
-entry rug
-another desk chair
-lights

Addresses of 2 places to donate used items

~

I believe in the apartment next to me lives a captive woman.
I believe I am a nun.
I believe I am being erased.
I believe Montréal will bury me without ceremony, just as they razed
the little hill when no longer needed to uphold their fort, the sacred hill
was destroyed because when something sacred no longer backs your
war it must be destroyed or it may rise in opposition.

~

Rum

Rum's message:
To you
From you
Fuck you.

~

I no longer hear my poetry voice in my head. Where the hell is it?
Buried under bread. I'm going back to bed.

My 51st birthday

The day starts late, as I've slept in again, the city's rhythm being so strong as to overtake my own. My new amie and I go to brunch at Maison Christian. On the way I see and wave to my neighbour with his new dog, and we exchange pleasantries. I am grateful to the stones and the sky and feel full of life in my new Denis Gagnon net with tunic over it.

I go to see the river. Habitat is stacked messily, and next to it, stacked neatly are some blue containers blowing a raspberry in its direction. On the ice a team of men push a racing boat with 1 foot in and 1 foot out for each of them, and seamlessly, miraculously, all jump into the boat when it reaches open water and within seconds are paddling in unison.

Yesterday, last day of their season, I did the zip line. Another amie is kind enough to film it, but mistakenly films the wrong person, so only a smudge of black, skirt billowing is me in the trees, and the photo is perfect—I felt like a witch on a broomstick, although quite frightened at first and at last, the ride in-between was exhilarating. Then she came and admired the condo and left a pile of croissant crumbs on the couch after our heart to heart talk about what one can say about messages from Nature without permission. Today I bought the painting "Undecided" and call her "The Leaf Priestess".
This is what contentment feels like.

DREAMS/
RÊVES

Writing poetry while waiting for other things to happen.

~

Warning

What if
instead of the highway warning us
about animals
"Moose"
Nature warned
"Asphalt"

~

It's cool and still except some tapping noise. I imagine a deer, the deer from Bagnolle and Bobbetts toy store, or from the past, walking delicately down the street, fresh washed from rain. The caution tape restless around the scissor lift, cones half hidden in shadow, glowing orange bright and orange dark like geometric partners to the spherical moon—quarter moon cones, their sun a streetlight. Tree's branch dances, and so does the red caution tape. I am the only one to see it.

Inspired by Leonard Cohen

"Welcome to these lines"
Welcome Bienvenue Gratitude
Kiss the stone and keep me grounded
When war is coming
Ships need anchors
and towns need walls
and you are pressed into services
as defense
as bulwark
as the bottom
under which is death
hold us up
upright
righteous
make us understand
we are the world
standing on the earth we protect
it is their prayer

Leonard would cry
Because I can't even imagine a world without war.
Stones are the real slaves
building European shelters on Indigenous lands
wishing to be left to their own ruminations
some at the edge of the sea

Montréal Musée des Lieux Perdues

I want to make the Montréal Musée of Lost Places (Lieux Perdue)

Inside would be the sacred hill
the French tore down after it was
no longer useful for the fort they built on it as an original desecration

Also inside or maybe circling around the building like a moat,
Little River that used to en-island the city
which they filled with sewage
then put underground because it was a health hazard

Next, the things they built and lost—
the walls of wood then earth and stone that protected the city
from those other Europeans
until they found a way in via trade
anyway.

Lastly, the wholes that are now in pieces—
the island where the stone came from that fronts these buildings
the Tribal Nations with their land and traditions intertwined
now with less of both

Maybe, too an afterthought
for those things they should take down now,
things they should lose
the cross on the hill
the statues of men with guns
the traditions that abrogate all rights to European-born humans
and everything
and everyone else
as resources to fulfill their needs.

The murdered and missing
Indigenous women haunt these streets.
Do the ghosts of Indigenous religions live with them, the collective
feminine of humans and of earth-based beliefs

lost and wandering in the snowflakes
as ephemeral/unreal/uninstantiated
swirling and as unfocussed as snow

Someone, a friend, a newly made friend of a spiritual bent
once called me a bright blue flame that lasers in and
a woman of balanced talents
but perhaps her version of me
melted over time too
because we hardly see one another anymore
and I no longer think she thinks of me that way
with respect and understanding
of any one part of me
the part inside that knew who I am
is in my own musée of lost places somewhere in a snow covered
wilderness
beyond that line of trees that Frost said marked the place
where he would not be lost
but more himself.

Murdered and Missing Indigenous Hill
(near intersection of Berri and Notre Dame)

Before they took the women
they signalled their intent
and took the sacred hill
mastectomy of the land

Her roundness reduced to resource

Yet....
the feminine
once again took hold
here

On the lookout promontory
a christian church
Our Lady gazing across the water
Your Lady unable to save you from the aggression of your brothers

Your women were murdered too

And Yet...
Now the Asian newcomers
pagan crones
walk to the far eastern point
colonized by monuments to western time
war cannons at its base—
and hold their palms up to greet the sun

—as you took the natural hill,
we take your unnatural terrace
made of the consecrated stone
and by our veneration
bring the sacred feminine of this place to life once again

Missing Concrete

He's the kind of man I always thought I would have
An urbane naturalized Eastern European
tall with an academic stoop, wild hair, expensive outré designer glasses
and a button down Oxford
a kind, refined manner that quickly turned sharp in the face of
stupidity, dullness, or bad behavior

The kind of man who knows how to take care of himself in the city
where to get the best bagels, sox, and antique pens
he lives in a booklined apartment in the heart of the old port
where he bought cheap before gentrification
with impeccable furniture
covered in papers
and a typewriter he uses every morning between 3-5am
while drinking Arabian coffee and carefully munching a croissant from
the corner bake shop (they open the door especially for him)

His novel, 700 pages, has been accepted by his friend, an editor at
Little and Brown
but he isn't happy with the ending and won't send the final draft until
he is.

His head of library job includes politics, budgeting, and erudite
conversation, at all of which he excels
his bow tie collection is legendary

He's never learned to drive
and to get to his seaside cottage (in the family since 1910) for his
month of summer vacation he takes a complicated and impeccably
orchestrated series of metro, bus, and ferry,
finally ritualistically walking the last mile in his soft brown shoes

Half way through the second week, on the wooden porch swing, he
looks up from his leather notebook
and realizes he misses concrete.

—

EPILOG

I won't be remembered—
I was never known.

AUTHOR BIOGRAPHY

Lis McLoughlin, PhD is the founder and director of NatureCulture® a publishing and events company through which she directs the Writing the Land® Project which pairs poets with conserved lands, and creates anthologies sold for land conservation. As of summer 2025, Lis works with over 350 poets and 150 land conservation organizations in the USA, Canada, Ireland, and the Cayman Islands, and has published 16 Writing the Land anthologies and 10 other books about Nature. She works at the intersection of arts, environment, and community, and holds annual international in-person writing retreats that seek to give back to the places they visit. Lis has degrees in Civil Engineering, Education, and Science and Technology Studies. She lives off-grid in Northfield, Massachusetts and in Montréal, Québec.

www.nature-culture.net   www.writingtheland.org

Photo: A. Riemenschneider

About NatureCulture®

The mission of NatureCulture® is to help humans be in right relationship with the rest of the natural world.

Please see all NatureCulture's publications at:
https://www.nature-culture.net

Other NatureCulture® Books

2025
Dark Matter: Women Witnessing, Dreams Before Extinction, eds. Weil, et al
The Nemo Poems: A Martian Perspective, by Rodger Martin
The Sleeping Dogs of Lubec, by Rodger Martin
Writing the Land: Rensselaer County, NY
Writing the Land: Horizons
Hoosic River, a poem by David Crews
Handfast, poems by Katherine Hagopian Berry
On Resiliance: Stories of Climate Adaptation Across Washington's Landscapes, by Morgan & Senechal, and WTL Poets

2024
The Black River: Death Poems ed. Deirdre Pulgram-Arthen
Cayman Brac From Bluff to Sea
Writing the Land: The Connecticut River
Writing the Land: Wanderings I
Writing the Land: Wanderings II
Writing the Land: Virginia
Wriring the Land: Maine II, A Gathering
Writing the Land: Northeast (2nd edition)

2023
Writing the Land: Youth Write the Land
Writing the Land: Currents
Writing the Land: Channels
Writing the Land: Streamlines
The Way of Gaia by Bridge & Trombulak
Migrations and Home: The Elements of Place, ed. Simon Wilson
From Root to Seed: Black, Brown, and Indigenous Poets Write the Northeast, ed. Samaa Abdurraqib

2022
Writing the Land: Foodways and Social Justice
Writing the Land: Windblown I
Writing the Land: Windblown II
Writing the Land: Maine
LandTrust, poems by Katherine Hagopian Berry

Forthcoming (2025-2027)
Writing the Land: The Cayman Islands
Writing the Land: Pathways
Writing the Land: The Great Forest of Aughty
Alex the Guardshark, by L. McLoughlin, & artwork by C.F. Morales